Internal Difference

David C. Ward is an historian at the National Portrait Gallery, Smithsonian Institution where he has curated exhibitions on Walt Whitman and Abraham Lincoln, among others. With graduate degrees from Warwick University and Yale, he is the author of *Charles Willson Peale. Art and Selfhood in the Early Republic* (2004) and (with Jonathan D. Katz) *Hide/Seek: Difference and Desire in American Portraiture* (2010).

T0096351

DAVID C. WARD

Internal Difference

tenth year
since my father's death
neighbors still quarreling

LINTOTT PRESS
Manchester and Glasgow

Acknowledgements

Many of these poems are published here for the first time. Others have previously appeared in *Aethlon*, *Connecticut River Review*, *Foolscap*, *Frogpond*, *Illuminations*, *London Quarterly*, *Metropolitain*, *Monocacy Valley Review*, *Plainsongs*, *Poem*, *Poetry Motel*, *PNReview*, *Potomac Review*, *Talking River Review* and *Wind*.

"*Def:* Extreme Rendition" was also produced as a limited edition, fine art broadside by the artist and printer Julio Granda and can be ordered by emailing wardd412@gmail.com.

"Colossus" was the basis for an art installation by Nekisha Durrett at the Hillyer Art Space, Washington DC, 2–31 October 2009.

Copyright © David C. Ward 2011-02-27

First published in Great Britain in 2011 by
Lintott Press
Manchester and Glasgow

ISBN 978 1 84777 162 9

Typeset by XL Publishing Services, Tiverton
Printed and bound in England by SRP Ltd, Exeter

For My Brothers

Chris and Andrew

where the meanings are

Contents

June, Swoon

Insomniacs know
The indifferent moon
Cares naught for you.

But it's always there
Just when you need it:
The tidal pull

At your blood and heart
A white page, a canvas
The pencil start.

Slake

Rest on your haunches
at stream side.
Cup your hands together.
Bow toward the further bank.
Balanced, dip your hands;
let the water fill the bowl
of your hands;
raise them from the water
without haste.

Drink from your bowled
hands. Bowing, drink again
from the cup you hold
in your hands. Rising,
cup your face
in your cooled hands.

Think of where
you have to go today.
Go there

Still we pretend at modesty

These days, dreams of modest heroism
cloud even the smallest tyrant's mind.
Who is exempt from self-effacing hubris?
No one is an erratic driver or a bad lover
when history is behind the wheel of fate.
We can't kid ourselves; we all acquiesce.
Everything is in play now as even quiet
moments down by the old mill pond
are a product placement opportunity. But
still we pretend at modesty even as we rise
like trout to plaudits which sting our mouths
with the ashes of electronic funds. Rinse, repeat:
was any complex civilization ever founded
on such a simple formulation?

                    So, Katy bar the door.
And if you're doing nothing tonight, please drop by?
We'll each keep a foot on the floor, like pool players,
and keep company for a while. You won't stay.
Who does these days? One (notice the distancing
pronoun) gets used to it. Yet alone or not, sometimes
in the waking dream of night, cutting the electric
chatter which now hums our synapses, I smell white
water and follow the tracery of rivers among cold pines.

No Place

It's hard to fathom anymore
with no more news from nowhere.
Quiet nostalgia is a frail reed to justify
lives lived to the rhythm of t.v. dinners
and traffic reports. The verities of weather
trouble us only on video while our lives
seal us up with air-born mites and molds.
Where did all these lung ailments come from
anyway? The pine scented fresheners
don't seem to work and wearied
by the ersatz sublime desperate measures
are required. At least by some.

                 Poor heart: no more Aeolian
strings humming the hyperbolic ether, a dynamo
gorgeously electrifying us in all our struggles
and up against which we were fierce in losing.
Now the thrum is all inside while our internal air
crusts up canals and channels, rimes our tear ducts
shut with salt. Erratically, a recurring dream breaks
through halcion day nights of sleep: A river
shimmers just beyond that near-distant scrim of trees.
So close, we could almost walk there if we would.

Surplus Value

My Michigan brother-in-law was a tool and die guy,
A machinist, fabricating parts in shops supplying Big Three
Auto makers. A bantam with thick fingers, scarred hands
He rode a Harley soft-tail, drank Iron City, and lived
With his wife and kids in a house he mostly built himself.
During the heyday of Detroit metal, overtime and union
Contracts paid for steaks and a cabin on an upstate lake
For summer vacations and deer season hunting trips
In the fall. He took his pride from his craft and skill
Building something bigger than the Fords or Chevys
He pushed on down the line for America to drive.
For twenty years of work, good times, and happy with it.
But that road ran out. The union went south first
(pension fraud; indictments; prison terms) and then
The companies and their money men slashed and burned
Their way through labor and its costs in search of market
Share. The work was sweated from the men for less and less return.
From economy of scale, to one of scarcity: subcontracting, piecework,
Ultimately the dole replaced a steady pay check and a bonus
Twice a year. The Harley went and then the cabin; food stamps
Bought essentials, nothing more. Always quiet, he grew quieter
From day to week to month to the years that stretched ahead,
Bowing his neck each day as the scars grew deeper now, and inward.

During the boom that no one thought would ever end,
Heedless the factories flushed their waste straight into
The Saginaw River, so much so that it never iced, even
In the depths of winter. Now it's frozen all year long.

Aces and Eights

Early mornings, two or three a.m., when my father couldn't sleep
He'd make his way downstairs and brew a coffee, black and bitter
To sit at the kitchen table with a pack of Luckies and a deck of cards,
Dealing out dummy poker hands, playing them himself against himself.
Five or seven card stud were his games; never draw, a game for kids,
He'd say, not a real man's game. Calculating odds and chances in his head,
He'd check and raise, hold and fold, spinning cards out in semicircular
Array to put them through their paces. Smoking all the while and sipping
From his cup, he'd impose his pattern on their random fall of meaning.
He'd learned to play, like most of the men of his generation, on football
Roadtrip bus rides and then continued in the War, breaking the monotony
Of hurry up and wait with an endless game of table stakes with cash
That it was bad luck to keep, a smaller gamble of one's luck against
The biggest cashing out of all. Cutthroat camaraderie that men learn
To relish, the poker games didn't long survive once middling age,
Professional aspirations and ultimate success, domesticated affluence
(a wife; three kids) took up all his time: no waiting now, all hurry.
Now dealing out the dummy hands was a vestigial routine, a way to fight
Another war, against the daily rote, the clock, and what he thought
He had become. A mindful mindlessness in which the fall of pasteboard
Squares filled the night's unease, keeping out the growing sense
That something somewhere had been lost somewhere back in time.
*

Outside the old Victorian in which we lived, the sky would begin to lighten,
He'd let the dogs out (they were his wife's in truth), and clean the ash tray
                                                            and coffee cup,
Taking time with rituals, filling each necessary day.

Relict

My great aunt Carlie (from Carlton, her family name)
despite Parkinson's and widow's weeds lived to be one hundred
and four years of age. Born in the Centennial year, 1876
she passed away in 1980, living alone in the Danvers Home
for the Aged and Infirm having outlived two husbands
(the first died in the 'flu epidemic of 1917, the second in 1952),
sons and daughters, assorted collateral kin, even her younger
sister, who only made it to ninety-four. Every Fourth of July
for a long time she rode in the town's Independence Day
parade, honored as Danvers' eldest citizen. A bright spark
to near the end and something of a ham, she loved waving
to the crowd from the back of a big boat Cadillac convertible,
the one with shark-like fins. As she aged her mind refused
to focus on the here and now but she kept a startling vision
of her father's sad decline from wealth to someone in the trade:
a disastrous turn of the century decision to back kerosene,
not gasoline. A not unfamiliar history, status thereafter derived
not from money or striving but from lineage: A family
and its place in time. Avid for genealogy she traced her family –
Putnams mostly – back to the Bay Colony, the Covenant, the
City on a Hill and all the history that could be spun out from
those first things. A teleology of grace and consolation
as the world passed the North Shore by. Her family – mine too –
had a window in Fanueil Hall, graves in the Old Granary,
were patriots who fought in one or another revolutionary battle
(the details were always somewhat imprecise) and formed
the backbone of the DAR and the Cincinnati, those momento
morii of a declining race. She never moved far from
those little towns, satellite to Boston's hub, sitting still
and calm as time washed in from somewhere else and left
her looking back, with a clearer sense of where it was she'd been.

Material Culture

Mute, wood breathes in but gives us nothing back
For all the years since someone made it into
Something else: a shape, a form, a purposed
Work of art that a family – in this case mine-
Bought and kept since it was made some time
In the 1750s north of Boston. Danvers or Salem
Craftsmen, anonymous but skilful men,
Took burled walnut and with practiced hands
Fit it to the tongue and groove of customary pattern,
Added brass fittings and set it out to catch the eye.
A slant front Chippendale, a desk just luxe enough
To signify a rising man but serious for the work at hand:
Merchant, lawyer, office holder. It's not known who
Bought it first but family legend pridefully maintains
General Israel Putnam – "Old Put" – who fought
With Washington, owned it once. There's a faded paper
That says so, so perhaps. But if its genealogy is intact
Albeit inexact, I want to know what it absorbed
In my family's travels from there and then to here and now.
But wood stands mute, breathing nothing back.

Drowning Narcissus

No, you're not in any especial danger.
Know you're not the center of the pool.
Realize that the blue gold blueness of the sky
is always racing indifferently away,
uncaring of whatever you're up to today
or any other day. Tear your gaze away
and follow on. Consider the orange.
Avoid old ventures requiring new shoes.
Learn how to shrug – eloquently –
while watching where you walk not how.
But use a plumb bob to fix your posture
and since fecklessness is the other side
of the old coin, keep a weather eye.
For good luck, tattoo a hex sign over
your heart. But above all else, cut
the chatter, especially to your self.
Prune vigorously, blending a new masque
from last year's gleanings. Cultivate
a different diction but don't expect results
in less than a lifetime. So take time
to fallow for a little while or a while longer.
Flow your sense of touch over the world's skin
and unstopper your ears. Try listening
through your eyes and turn down the light
level of the noise. Consider yourself as
a net that gives back its takings –
know which is which and stay off the median.
Separate your body from yourself,
like skin from fruit from pith from essence.

Peel the orange.
Release it into someone else's dreams.

The River Refuses its Name

On the 400th anniversary of Henry Hudson's discovery of the Hudson River

The river was the river's before it was ours.
Pull back and see it as it was. Reverse the flow
Of time and unpeel our landscape from the land.
Take the names and maps away: the incised grid
Of highway, road, and bridge; the connective tissue
That gives a motion to our lives. Take away the imprint
Of the names we give to place and time:
This landmark, or that battle,
This statesman or that conglomerate
From overseas. The markings that we make
In all our ceaseless commerce in the world. The walls
Of glass, the city's tunnels warrened underground,
And the restless bedlam shriek of all the dailiness
That keeps our lives afloat in what we know
As life. Modern times canyoning its heedless way
Through all our pasts and all we think we can control.
So thus the reassurance that we get from naming things
To get some fictive grip on all we think we've learned
Or know, a sense of where we've been and where we go,
The habitual views that we pass by each day
Distracting us in custom's groove and rote
From what is now and what we've never really seen.

So start over. Think beyond ourselves
This time and all that we kept out by all our putting in.
Go back to see the river as it was before we started time.
Don't think of the river as ourselves.
Don't think of the river as our history.
Don't think of the river as anything but the river:
Cold, whole, inviolate, merciless in the integrity
Of its ceaseless mountainous riverflow.

Jackson Pollock Crashes His Car

gear shift slicks
tonguing tires into smoke
obscured neon
bruising the black
night light sky
reflected in oil
stained panties riding
shotgun in a Detroit lean
hard chasing stars
splashed high
above cat feet fogged
road slide-ruled
plumb through trees
rushing past to midnight's
zipper tear screams
chroming mouths
slack with idle
salt pooling lip-ward
in a gulp of wind-
ing air turning
to silence spinning
wheels in chords
unheard among desperate
spheres in ether
frozen dreams westing
back to zero
white canvas glaring

Two San Francisco Poets

Weldon Kees' Car

was found by a cop on the beat
at 2am in a park near the Golden Gate,
the doors and windows open, fog tendrils
blowing – an easy metaphor picked up
by literary detectives trying to fathom
Kees' unexplained, shocking vanishing.
The law assumed suicide or "death by misadventure,"
empty car plus proximity to the suicide bridge
added up to a familiar story. Case closed. But no
body was ever found and years later a journalist
claimed to have seen Kees somewhere down
in Mexico – probably in the same town where JFK
hangs out with Marilyn and Elvis (slim again) plays
hillbilly guitar. The reporter said Kees ducked him
And disavowed all knowledge of the arts.
Other sightings have been made, all unconfirmed.
Weldon Kees: painter, poet, specter of what
might have been. When he got lost he had
a growing reputation. He desired none.

Jack Spicer

kept a bottle always handy to drown
the words that streamed incessantly
through him like the jolt from an electric chair.
A student of linguistic theory, he concocted
a theory – unprovable, disparaged, incomplete –
that we are but like radio receivers for a language
beamed in from somewhere else. A passive
antennae, he tried to order all the chaotic words
streaming through his appalled and unsuspecting
mind, an incessant fizzing overload that froze his will.
Gripped in a logos he could not comprehend,
he gibbered, spoke ecstatically. People shied away.
Tortured for years, he finally flipped the switch,
drank himself to death and at the end diagnosed
himself precisely: "My vocabulary did this to me."

Camouflage Self-Portrait

In 1987, aged fifty-nine Andy Warhol bored
and played out in the modern life he made
(after the first lunch with Jackie O/there is no other)
faked his own death – routine gallbladder procedure:
gone awry – slipped quietly from the hospital
back into his mother's house, his Pittsburgh boyhood
home. Wig gone, black suit and fancy glasses trashed,
he donned the clothes and life of a nondescript ordinary
working man, took a bakery assistant's job making crullers
and cakes, introduced himself as Stosh from somewhere
vaguely somewhere else, and joined the local bowling
league. He learned to polka at the Legion Hall, amiably
fending off the local widows, and grew quietly old alone.
He cooked for one and after dinner would sit and watch
as the neighborhood wound down from dusk to night.
He developed a real fondness for baseball:
                    it was so slow.

Myriads of Eternity

Two-deckers backed against thruways and rail freight
Shunting yards; cars go by all day. The light
Stanchions of the old ball park crane above the flat
Roof line after line of brick row houses. Meanly portioned
Backyard spaces done up as best one can: grass and garden plots,
Flowers bend to the chemical gauze filtering yellow light.
Front door stoops, two concrete slab steps whitewashed yearly,
Soap scrubbed weekly against the bellying smoke stack clouds.

At street corners, taverns and ill stocked grocery stores,
Bus stops where at 5 a.m. men with broken feet, cracked hands
Wait stiff in coveralls for the day to start. The arriving buses
Carry back women who work as chars downtown at night in office
Jobs. Now they hardly run at all. Work's will be done.

Saints Today

The frame
of poverty, cracked
paint and water
marked.
Wreckage. The good
intentions
gone awry
beaten like a
rug you lie
bewildered
by the size
of what's beyond
your door.
Receding fast,
life leaks
away
like tears of blood
from daily
arrows.

Internal Difference

The air thick with years of chalk motes
Acrid, cutting the damp wool fug of winter coats
Pegged in a line along one wall. Schoolchildren
Serried in old fashioned seats and fliptop desks
Bow heads to their teacher or to something anyway.
Among them an ordinary boy quiet in chain store
Corduroy: a nondescript, adrift in more than lessons
The taste of sour milk fills his mouth.

No schoolchildren triggered reveries here
Then in the greying hour now before the alarm.
Forty years on in my eye's mind I am doubled back
Into and outside myself, at once familiar and
A distant other to my current self: Impossible
To – yet impossible not to wish to – retrieve
The intervening time rising once before my own
Small distant figure, irredeemable across the climb.

*

The clock trips over, begins its electronic rasp,
As if time was starting up again.

Teleology

Wouldn't everything have been a lot easier
    if: Arriving at the terminal
the lovers missed each other, and wandered
    aimless in the crowds until,
one waiting in the bar, the other leafing magazines
    they both picked up casual
conversations with strangers which quickly moved
    with an audible click,
brushing a lock of hair, having a second drink,
    to something else, from which
brush contact they both danced slowly and then
    suddenly into long loves full
of children and delight. Thus forestalling the
    inevitable slow slough of boredom
and middle-class routine – ennui with adultery,
    outbreaks of broken crockery –
for which a dyspeptic not too attentive God marked them.
    So that years later both
tried to recall who it was they were to meet that day
    but gave up with a laugh
after a thought's flicker to make dinner and love.

Instead, time unrolled for them as for empires:
    drawn through the crowd
ineluctably they met and in a second fell.

Simple Explanation

After twenty-one years –

    one wife, prettily plump and supportive with a slight
                tendency to psychobabble
    one child, who took after her mother and sang in choir
    two dogs, one unmanageable
    one car, one cliched van of suburban yuppiedom
    big tract house, with deck and hot tub add ons
    little lake side cottage, with deck for night time twinings
    some hobbies, and
    a job selling things gladhanded on the road –

he just left, a leaving which left in its one act drama's wake

much commentary:
bewildered cries and general censure,

    (except for the unmanageable dog
    who, fed twice daily, never noticed)

from neighbors and friends, at work and home
and was followed by the tortured exegises of
therapists and lawyers parsing love and money.
And throughout, Occam's razor cut too deep
for anyone to dare unfold it:

    He hated how his life
    had become exterior
    through and through
    like a wound.

For those who hear what we cannot

The madman, skirled at dusk by a late
       autumn wind, sits cricked on a stone bench
Knee balancing a typewriter in his mind.
       An old Royal beater perched on the pullout ledge
Of a yard sale yet varnished study desk
       in a cone of lambent yellow suspended
Alongside shelves and stacks of file-cards folders
       notebooks teetering from accreted marshalled
Ordered facts. Material bulked to fill out others'
       past and his present lives,
Establishing an order his own fragile self cannot maintain.
       Fallen now through the study's floor
Outside in the strange angled November light
       He hunches, hammering down each fictive page
Elbows beating like a diving seabird's wings
       Thrashing away at darkness. Into light.

Isn't It Pretty to Think So?

Fathers playing catch
with sons:
American as wheatfields mown
into ball fields
around which
great cities are built and on which
a golden light still
congregates
undimmed.

This father
playing catch with
this son: a stinging rebuke
sizzles in over
and over again, stitches thrumming
redly, welting a child's plam
from palm through arm to blood fogged brain.
Pitching with intent: "Come on!
Be a Man!"

I want to learn
and not be told and then have that telling
gilded in a
myth which smothers our unease
over beaten fathers
beating sons.

The Sublime Meets Prairie Town

Rain stops down the street
signals left and rolls
on, sheeting the town
from stem to stern, obscuring
the air with the false
promise of thunder heads
and change. Squalls don't
shift the shape of things
long enough to matter.
All style, sublime foreboding
never delivers its electric
promise.
      Quickly, sugar beet
fields, water towers, angle parked
trucks outside main street
stores, luncheon counters
and threshers starting up again
re-emerge from rain's distancing
sepia. Clouds roll away,
uncovering the constant line
of space and plain.
      The horizon glares
her eye as the storm winks out
its promise. She runs the laundry
out again across the drying yard.
Sheets billow. The line pulleys out,
endlessly returning to her constant hand.

Jamais Vu or Was It?

Seductive is the easy elegy
to the way things never were.
This porch, that swing,
a child's first crush, buzz of bees.
At dusk, parabolas of skipping ropes
and baseballs looped from boy's arm
to dad's hand. Deep in chairs, adults murmur
what adults murmur at days end.
Always, a melancholy sense of something
coming on that never quite arrives.
Life becoming the apprehension
of all its ordinary beauty, a kaleidoscope
with no surprises in the resolution of
shape and form at each day's shaking.

That's not the way it was you say
And you are, of course, exactly right.
Dad got bitter after a drink or three
and muttered about missed chances.
Mother cried unnervingly at sudden times.
The Russians stole the Bomb and Emmitt
Till was lynched. That girl never
liked me after all and the grass was
always patchy brown by June.

Except it was exactly how we think it was.
The past is how we've learned to face
each day's tidal pull. We stitch the pattern
up around our selves until it fits
a second skin. What should have been
becomes what was, what is. Our lives
become a facing we display to structure selves
so chancy and so frail, that one look's
honest touch would break them into shards.
History isn't written by the victors
but each day's victims, day after every day.

Inheritance

In brightness's middle
a shadow falls,
                shearing garden's light
to shade.

A surprise of tears
                blurs me
back to my father's suits, the blue and grey
        of his lost cause.

We only ever spoke in code
                      of things
until the code became ourselves, all
meaning lost and darkness

wrapped round our tongues like shrouds –

        binds me still.

Angle of Deflection

The ironic voice works well for scholars
     in their seminars and preceptorials.
Played in a muted tone it provides

A mask of cool engagement for the
     parsing of ideas, the teasing out of meanings.
     The teacher as ironist is antithesis:

Half-glasses edging down as an up-from under
     peering look of inquisition asks for
clarity from the passionate and elaboration
From the hesitant; in withdrawal, others are drawn forward.
     interventions are asides: A quick tight snaggled grin,
a fissure of pleasured empathy rewards

A gridwork of connections constructed and revealed.
     a stab of the ashtray (the cigarette as sign; discuss) marks
the summing up, the gathering of chords, and,

In patterned ineluctable sequence, the close of one meeting
     the opening of the next.

As a scholar, the ironic voice works well for you:
     You win prizes for your teaching.
But, too subtle an ironist, your engagement is its
     opposite. And it is not a style.

Removed from the teleology of unfolding syllabi
     can you put the mask aside, connect?

Still Life, Grand Central Station

Buy the premise and you buy the drink
the glittering bottled landscape
of your dreams. Set ups – setting out –
shiny and bright rainbow of glass and ice
– olives and pearl onions – swank the bar
as westward the course of empire takes your sway.
Just one quick pop before the train
its bullet blows right through your brain
and stains your shirt with what is just beyond,
the shards of presque-vue. The what of what
has almost been. Doubled, in the mirror something flicks,
a trout across a too clear pool: too quick to grasp
except in recognition that it's past. You almost held
it once but now it's down to white nights and t.v.,
the finality of women's heels, hissing phones.
Office walls are gray to match your fate,
the calendar unchanging, time in spate.

Alcool

Remember the flaring
manic nights, the crackle
riding shotgun to the dawn.
The quiet first sip in the still lit bar
or the first one of the day:
The necessary glow of glass.

Not the after wreck. Time and future
all holed out. The disappeared:
this job, those friends, a family
somewhere else. Not the spittle
flecks and the snake's tongue
flicking out.

Carpal Tunnel Syndrome

Hammered between nine and the anvil
five, keystrokes dice the day finer than
any razor. Half-hour for lunch, two quarter
hour breaks, toilet privileges (waste not want
not a new job) a privilege now. Work
rates of the networked bartlebys flash
like pulselines on overseers' monitors:
Keep up to speed or you'll disappear.

The division of labor once broke whole
bodies down from the skin side in, now
it insinuates from tiny nerve ends out.
The end's the same: life cut down to dust.

Marginalia

Presto! the cabinet flourishes,
the bikini babe jumps out restored, no longer sliced in two.
Sleight of hand works
only for other people who effortlessly pluck
the ace from a bloom of doves. In your case, feet
metastasize, bulging your swaybacked boots like hydroponic
artichokes. Collars tightening
with each day's alarum, grindstones sharpen to a dull nub
no oil can smooth. Years.
Meanwhile, success is for someone else who
yet against the forensics sees himself as on a fringe
arms flailing, a fat man wandering on thinning ice, wondering
how the milk got on *your* whiskers.

Call Waiting. Waiting...

Exurban lawns green slick with
grass emollients. Computer plantings. A blow-in from the arctic
turns, bemused, heading out, with nicitating eyes.
Barbecue grills, chefs with funny hats
and aprons (assembly lined, is a joke a joke?), briquet
a darkness, scrumbling the dusk's light.
No election news fizzes
through the ether as hearts go south. No surfing here.
Wood and brick click, the invisible tick of atom clocks
notching the changes until the stirrup snaps, extinguishing
close hearing, small sounds. And then animals run
across thinning slates roofing detached
houses. Their thrumming paws
rip like Ringo on a roll. Adulteries, arranged by phone
kept by rote, mechanical, a groove
of 4/4 time. Regular as the news.

Canker

Gray black beforelight,
Goya's skalls and chavs,
all beaky and socket-eyed,
humped by cloak and bag,
chivvy the KIA splayed naked,
clothes, boots and arms long looted,
out on some Spanish steppe.
Raping the dead: pliering teeth,
snipping the rare ring or locket,
turning away with a shuffled kick
to the balls or after a casual piss,
splattering a hole, once a mouth.

Christmas dawn 1999.
Amidst fluorescent dread, infarcted
by muzaked carols, piss cutting germicides,
my mother dies
and, scuttling quickly, Staff crabs
through her effects, divvying
whilst her wispy corpse is swabbed
and bagged, parceled for chambering.
On complaint, Hospital shrugs
prize winning shoulders, yawns, piles
on more forms. After all, it was really
just junk really, a watch and stuff
– a brooch, a photo frame, a wedding band—
no one – not her! – will ever really miss.

In afterlight's odd forgetful hours
I tongue the empty socket in my jaw
honoring the unknown dead.

Bone Cold

Out in the December bitter churchyard
The wind is barely broken by the wall and stones.
Huddled warmth impossible to find as the
Offices are performed: a chapped exhalation of
Icy breath and the words are whipped away.
The eye drawn blinkingly to the luminescent
Rug of astroturf carefully arranged out of some
Absurd propriety to hide the mound of fresh turned earth
As if there were no holes to fill.

The shock of pain pulses steadily now like a vein.
What was barely to be borne inhabits you like the wind.

Clothes Make the Man

After my father died the chores
    of death were done
until nothing but his clothes
    remained. I stood,
my mother out walking with the dogs,
    at his closet going
through a life in cloth. From fifties'
    vanilla conformity,
demobilized khaki, academic corduroy,
    an ascending arc
of a career, gravitas stitched out
    in suits and ties
of finer text, more subtle hues; we
    buried him in his best.
And as the cloth rippled, bespoke waves
    under my casual hands
a flicker of greed licked out: we were
    at least I thought
same sized, why let such rich things waste?
    I admired a broadcloth
three piece banker's stripe up against
    my chest and as I did
I caught not just my father's overt scent
    of bay rum and pomade
but a tracery of something deeper, fine
    woven in the cloth.
I put the jacket at my face to unforewarned
    go under at the sudden
cordite stink of all his working life.
    Ambushed, I could
not breathe again until all the hangers
    swung like ruined gallows.

Not Enough Room to Swing a Cat

As insomniac curtains billow, the certainty
that local knowledge is always wrong: that dowsing
by the old mill wall fonts no springs to flower
a fruited plain of jars.
That that whittler on the porch will always
send you a way so wrong it's almost right until the end
when ambush rattles
choke-mouthed through the fonds. Dry mouthed
prairies roll away to postoffice murals painted by the yard
of hardpack with a statue to the pioneers, or something like them anyway.
Who wants to think what life is really like?
Better to follow the curtain's flourish up and out beyond
to where mountains shout and July snow promises above trees.
Mystic to the end, the road hangs heavy, draping the horizon,
heading south. Or is it east? Anywhere so long
as out of Dodge and its entangling appliances.
Fuschia is the wedding color of the year. Next season black will be in style
and reversed boots.

At 9:45 a.m.

on 9/11, as we know it now,
Gene Smith, coming back from the dentist,
walks up the subway stairs
out into the skirling dust of History.

Thinking of his family, calculating,
he turns with the crowd,
walks north to the Terminal
and gets on the first bus heading out.

One year later, on the dot,
Gene Smith, in short sleeves
and a careful smile, walks to work
in the town of M_____, state of I_____.

Back in Bayside, his widow,
hollowed by the mourning rote,
touches their son's hand to the graven
name and years: closure of a sort.

Colossus

He knew what he knew
and did not know
what he did not know
which was
America.

The city
The hill
The river:
all a blank
in his one eyed mind.

His voice silted
the city's streets
flattened the hill
stilled the river flow
to his gray resolve.

The bread
no longer the body.
The wine
no longer the body.
The body

no longer the body.
The horn's bell
mute, full of dry
and bitter
fruit.

He knew what he knew
and did not know
what he knew
was not
America.

Def: *Extreme Rendition*

Rendition   The handing over of a fugitive
Or some other party
Of interest to the duly constituted
Authority of the State
Or his representative.'

Rendition   A surrender; a submission:
A bringing –
To the knees.
A bagging of the head
And eyes – the state
Of nullity.

Rendition   Sing me the song
That's why you're here
Give me the stuff
We want to hear.
Spiel me the tune boy
And you might
Stay o.k. but you know
What happens
If you don't want to play.

Render   Tear skin from flesh
Break bone
Break
And boil, reduce to grease.
Re-heat. Repeat
As necessary and desired.

Render   Unto Caesar –
Or eat the thorns –

Render   End Here. Enter Here.

The End of History

The knife, worn, sharpened to a mercy,
Poised tight on the son's jugular,
The neck offered, right knee pushing
The boy's back, left hand cupping
The boy's eyes, pulling back
Against the knee braced in the
Boy's back. Eternity holds the pose.

Sun sliding down, time starts:
The father's eyes filling with salt
The boy pissing himself
The knife slipping
Slicing a shark red wake
To splash the naked rock.

Where is the Angel now?